DANIEL THE PROPHET

BY

D. L. MOODY.

Fredonia Books
Amsterdam, The Netherlands

Daniel the Prophet

by
Dwight L. Moody

ISBN: 1-4101-0275-0

Fredonia Books
Amsterdam, The Netherlands
http://www.fredoniabooks.com

CONTENTS.

DANIEL'S BAND.

STANDING by a purpose true,
 Heeding God's command,
Honor them, the faithful few !
 All hail to Daniel's Band !

> Dare to be a Daniel !
> Dare to stand alone !
> Dare to have a purpose firm,
> Dare to make it known !

Many mighty men are lost,
 Daring not to stand,
Who for God had been a host,
 By joining Daniel's Band.

Many giants, great and tall,
 Stalking through the land,
Headlong to the earth would fall,
 If met by Daniel's Band !

Hold the Gospel banner high !
 On to victory grand !
Satan and his host defy,
 And shout for Daniel's Band !

P. P. BLISS

DANIEL THE PROPHET.

I.

THE CAPTIVES IN BABYLON.

"But Daniel purposed in his heart that he would not defile himself
with the portion of the king's meat, nor with the wine which he
drank ; therefore he requested of the prince of the eunuchs that he
might not defile himself" (Dan. i. 8).

ALWAYS delight to study the life of "Daniel the
Prophet." The name DANIEL means "God is
my judge." God is my judge : not the public is
my judge ; not my fellow-men, but God. So
Daniel held himself responsible to God. Some may ask, Who
was Daniel ? Listen. About six hundred years before the
time of Christ, the sins of the kings of Judah had brought
down upon them and upon the people the judgments of God.
Jehoiakim had succeeded Jehoahaz ; and Jehoiachin had succeeded Jehoiakim ; and he again was succeeded by Zedekiah ;
and of each of these kings the record runs just the same : " he
did evil in the sight of the Lord."

No wonder that in the days of Jehoiakim, about six hun-
drє d years before the time of Christ, Nebuchadnezzar, King of
Babylon, was permitted of God to come up against Jerusalem,
and to lay siege against it and overcome it. It was probably

at this time that Daniel, with some of the young princes, was carried away captive. A few years later, Jehoiachin being king, Nebuchadnezzar again came up against Jerusalem, and overcame it; when he bare away many of the temple vessels, and made several thousand captives.

And still later on, when Zedekiah was king, Nebuchadnezzar came a third time against Jerusalem to besiege it; and this time he burnt the city with fire; broke down its walls; slaughtered many of the people; and probably bore away another batch of captives to the banks of the Euphrates.

Among the earlier captives taken by the King of Babylon in the days of Jehoiakim, were four young men. Like Timothy in later times, they may have had godly mothers, who taught them the law of the Lord. Or they may perhaps have been touched by the words of Jeremiah, the "weeping prophet," whom God had sent to the people of Judah. So, when the nation was rejecting the God of Israel, the God of Abraham, of Isaac, and of Moses, these young men took Him as their God: they received Him into their hearts.

Many may have mocked at Jeremiah's warnings, when he lifted up his voice against the sins of the people; they may have laughed at his tears, and have told him to his face— just as people say nowadays of earnest preachers—that he was causing undue excitement. But these four young men would seem to have listened to the prophet's voice; and they had the strength to come out for God.

And now they are in Babylon. Nebuchadnezzar the king commands that a certain number of the most promising of the young Jewish captives should be picked out, who might be taught the Chaldean tongue and instructed in the learning of Babylon. And the king further ordered that there should be daily set before them portions of meat from his table, and a supply of the same wine as he himself drank; and this was to go on for three years. And at the end of three years these young men were to stand before the great monarch, at that time the ruler over the whole world. Daniel and his three young friends were amongst those thus selected.

No young man ever goes from a country home to a large city—say, to a great metropolis—without grave temptations crossing his path on his entrance. And just at this turning-point in his life, as in Daniel's, must lie the secret of his success or his failure. The cause of many of the failures that we see in life is, that men do not start right. Now, this young man started right. He took a character with him up to Babylon; and he was not ashamed of the religion of his mother and his father. He was not ashamed of the God of the Bible. Up there among those heathen idolaters he was not ashamed to let his light shine. The young Hebrew captive took his stand for God as he entered the gate of Babylon, and doubtless he cried to God to keep him steadfast. And he needed to cry hard, for he had to face great difficulties : as we shall see.

Soon comes a testing time. The king's edict goes forth, that these young men should eat the meat from the king's table. Some of that food would in all probability consist of meats prohibited by the Levitical law—the flesh of animals, of birds, and of fishes, which had been pronounced "unclean," and were consequently forbidden: or in the preparation, some portion might not perhaps have been thoroughly drained of the blood, concerning which it had been declared, " Ye shall eat the blood of no manner of flesh"; or some part of the food may have been presented as an offering to Bel or some other Babylonish god. Some one of these circumstances, or possibly all of them united, may have determined Daniel's course of action. I do not think it took young Daniel long to make up his mind. " He purposed in his heart "—IN HIS HEART, mark that !—"that he would not defile himself with the portion of the king's meat."

If some modern Christians could have advised Daniel, they would have said, " Do not act like that; do not set aside the king's meat: that is an act of Pharisaism. The moment you take your stand, and say you will not' eat it, you say in effect that you are better than other people." Oh, yes; that is the kind of talk too often heard now. Men say, " When you are in Rome you must do as Rome does;" and such people would have pressed upon the poor young captive that, though he might obey the commandments of God while in his own country, yet that he could not possibly do so here in Babylon —that he could not expect to carry his religion with him into the land of his captivity. I can imagine men saying to Daniel, " Look here, young man, you are too puritanical. Don't be too particular; don't have too many religious scruples. Bear in mind you are not now in Jerusalem. You will have to get over these notions, now you are here in Babylon. You are not now surrounded by friends and relatives. You are not a Jerusalem prince now. You are not surrounded by the royal family of Judah. You have been brought down from your high position. You are now a captive. And if the monarch hears about your refusing to eat the same kind of meat that he eats, and to drink the same kind of wine that he drinks, your head will soon roll from off your shoulders. You had better be a little politic."

But this young man had piety and religion deep down in his heart: and that is the right place for it; that is where it will grow; that is where it will have power; that is where it will regulate the life. Daniel had not joined the company of the "church," the faithful few in Jerusalem—because he wanted to get into "society," and attain a position : that was not the reason. It was because of the love he had toward the Lord God of Israel.

I can imagine the astonishment of that officer, Melzar, when Daniel told him he could not eat the king's meat or drink his wine. "Why, what do you mean? Is there any-thing wrong with it? Why, it is the best the land can pro-duce!"

"No," says Daniel, "there is nothing wrong with it in that way; but take it away, I cannot eat it." Then Melzar tried to reason Daniel out of his scruples; but no, there stood the prophet, youth though he was at that time, firm as a rock.

So, thank God, this young Hebrew and his three friends said they would not eat the meat or drink the wine; and requesting that the portions might be taken away, they endea-voured to persuade the overseer to bring them pulse instead.

"Take away this wine, and take away this meat. Give us pulse and water." The prince of the eunuchs probably trem-bled for the consequences. But, yielding to their importunity, he eventually consented to let them have pulse and water for ten days. And lo! at the end of the ten days his fears were dispelled; for the faces of Daniel and his young friends were fairer and fatter than the faces of any of those who had partaken of the king's meat. The four young men had not noses, like those of too many men nowadays seen in our streets, as red as if they were just going to blossom. It is God's truth—and Daniel and his friends tested it—that cold water, with a clear conscience, is better than wine. They had a clear conscience; and the smile of God was upon them. The Lord had blessed their obedience, and the four Hebrew youths were allowed to have their own way; and in God's time they were brought into favour, not only with the officer set over them, but with the court and the king.

Daniel thought more of his principles than he did of earthly honour, or the esteem of men. Right was right with him. He was going to do right TO-DAY, and let the morrows take care of themselves. That firmness of purpose, in the strength of God, was the secret of his success. **Right** there, that very moment, he overcame. And from that hour, from that moment, he could go on conquering and to conquer, because he had started right.

Many a man is lost because he does not start right. He makes a bad start. A young man comes from his country home, and enters upon city life: temptation arises, and he becomes false to his principles. He meets with some scoffing, sneering man, who jeers at him because he goes to a church service; or because he is seen reading his Bible; or because he is known to pray to God—to that God to whom Daniel prayed in Babylon. And the young man proves to be weak-kneed: he cannot stand the scoffs, and the sneers, and the jeers, of his companions; and so he becomes untrue to his principles, and gives them up.

I want to say here to young men, that when a young man makes a wrong start, in ninety-nine cases out of a hundred it is ruin to him. The first game of chance; the first betting transaction; the first false entry in the books; the first quarter-dollar taken from the cash-box or the till; the first night spent in evil company—either of these may prove the turning-point; either of these may represent a wrong start.

If ever any persons could be said to have had a good excuse for being unfaithful to their principles, these four young men might. They had been torn away from the associations of their childhood and their youth; had been taken away from the religious influences which centred in Jerusalem, away from the temple services and sacrifices; and had been put down in Babylon among the idols and idolaters, among the wise men and soothsayers, and the whole nation was against them. They went right against the current of the whole world.

BUT GOD WAS WITH THEM.

And when a man, for the sake of principle and conscience, goes against the current of the whole world, God is with him;

and he need not stop to consider what the consequences will be. Right is right.

But our testimony for God is not limited to a single act : it has to last all through our lives. So we must not imagine for a moment that Daniel had only one trial to undergo. The word to the Lord's servants is the same in all ages, " Be thou faithful *unto death.*"

This city of Babylon was a vast place. I suppose it to have been the largest city the world has ever seen. It is said to have been sixty miles round, and is understood to have consisted of an area of two hundred square miles.* A line drawn through the city in either direction would measure fifteen miles. The walls are said to have had an elevation of three hundred and fifty feet : they would therefore be nearly on a level with the dome of St. Paul's Cathedral. The breadth of the walls is said to have been over eighty feet, and on the top eight chariots could run abreast. Babylon was like Chicago—so flat, that for ornamentation men had to construct artificial mounds ; and, like Chicago in another particular, the products of vast regions flowed right into and through it.

* "Herodotus gives the circumference of Babylon as sixty miles ; the whole forming a quadrangle, of which each side was fifteen miles. M. Oppert confirms this by examinations on the spot, which show an area within the walls of two hundred square miles" (*Fausset's Bible Cyclopædia, p.* 67). A clearer idea of the enormous extent of Babylon will be formed if we understand that it probably occupied an area nearly *double* the extent of modern London. It must not, however, be supposed that Babylon contained a population comparable with that of London in point of numbers. The inhabitants of the former city probably numbered 1,200,000.

II.

"*THOU ART THE HEAD OF GOLD!*"

"Nebuchadnezzar dreamed dreams, wherewith his spirit was troubled, and his sleep brake from him" (Dan. ii. 1).

E hear of Daniel again some few years later on, and under new conditions. The King of Babylon had a dream ; and his dream greatly disturbed him. He musters before him the magicians, the astrologers, the soothsayers, and the Chaldæans (or learned men), and requires from them the interpretation of this night-vision of his. He either cannot or will not narrate to them the incidents of the vision, but demands an explanation without detailing what he had seen in his dream. "The thing is gone from me : if ye will not make known unto me the dream, with the interpretation thereof, ye shall be cut in pieces, and your houses shall be made a dunghill."

That was a pretty unreasonable demand. It is true that he offered them rewards and honours if they succeeded. But of course they failed. And they admitted their failure. "There is not a man upon the earth that can show the king's matter : therefore there is no king, lord, nor ruler that asked such things of any magician, astrologer, or Chaldean. And it is a rare thing that the king requireth ; and there is none other that can show it before the king, except the gods, whose dwelling is not with men."

"Except the gods." They did not mean the God of heaven—Daniel's God. He could have revealed the secret quick enough. They meant the idol-gods of Babylon, with whom these so-called "wise men" thought, and wrongly thought, the power of interpretation lay.

"There is not a man upon the earth that can show the king's matter." They were wrong there; and that they soon found out. "The king was angry and very furious, and commanded to destroy all the wise men of Babylon; and the decree went forth that the wise men should be slain; and they sought Daniel and his fellows to be slain."

The king's officer came to Daniel; but Daniel was not afraid. Says the officer to him, "You are classed among the wise men; and our orders are to take you out and execute you." "Well," says the young Hebrew captive, "the king has been very hasty. But let him only give me a little time; and I will show the interpretation."

He had read the law of Moses; and he was one of those who believed that what Moses had written concerning secret things was true: "The secret things belong unto the Lord our God; but the things that are revealed belong unto us, and to our children." He probably said to himself, "My God knows that secret; and I will trust to Him to reveal it to me." And he may have called together his three friends; and have held a prayer-meeting—perhaps the first prayer-meeting ever held in Babylon. They dealt with the threatening message of the King of Babylon just as Hezekiah had dealt with the threatening letter of the King of Assyria a hundred years before. They "spread it before the Lord." And they prayed that this secret might be revealed to them. And after they had prayed, and made their request to God—and the answer did not come right off, then and there—they went off to bed, and fell asleep.

I do not think that you or I would have slept much, if we had thought that our heads were in danger of coming off in the morning. Daniel slept: for we are told the matter was revealed to him in a dream or night-vision. Daniel's faith was strong: so he could sleep calmly in the prospect of death. If his friends did not sleep through the night it is most likely they were praying.

DANIEL STANDS BEFORE THE KING.

In the morning Daniel pours out his heart in thanksgiving. He "blessed the God of heaven" He had got into the spirit of Psalm ciii. : "Bless the Lord, O my soul, and all that is within me, bless His holy name!" Paul and Silas had the same spirit of thanksgiving when they were in the prison at Philippi. Daniel makes his way to the palace, goes into the guard-room, and says to the officer: "Bring me in before the king; and I will show unto the king the interpretation." He stands in the presence of Nebuchadnezzar; and, like Joseph before Pharaoh, before proceeding to unfold the dream, he gives glory to God : "There is a God in heaven that revealeth secrets." Daniel took his place as nobody : he himself was nothing. He did not wish the king to think highly of him. That is the very highest type of piety—when a man hides himself, as it were, out of the way ; and seeks to exalt his God and lift up his Redeemer, and not himself. And then he proceeds to describe the dream : "Thou, O king, sawest; and behold, a great image! This great image, whose brightness was excellent, stood before thee; and the form thereof was terrible."

I can imagine how the king's eyes flashed out at those opening words; and I can fancy him crying out, "Yes, that is it : the whole thing comes back to me now."

"This image's head was of fine gold; his breast and his arms of silver; his belly and his thighs of brass; his legs of iron ; his feet, part of iron and part of clay."

"Yes. that is it exactly," says the king; "I recollect all that now. But surely there was something more."

And Daniel goes on : "Thou sawest till that **a stone was**

cut out without hands, which smote the image upon his feet that were of iron and clay, and brake them to pieces. . . . This is the dream : and we will tell the interpretation thereof before the king."

And then, amidst death-like stillness, Daniel went on to unfold the interpretation ; and he told the king that the golden head of the great image was none other than himself. " Thou art this head of gold ! " He then goes on to tell of another kingdom that should arise—not so beautiful, but stronger ; as silver is stronger than gold : that described the Medo-Persian empire. But the arms of silver were to overthrow the head of gold. And Daniel himself lived to see the day when that part of the prophetic dream came to pass. He lived to see Cyrus overthrow the Chaldæan power. He lived to see the sceptre of empire pass into the hands of the Medes and Persians. And after them came a mighty Grecian conqueror, Alexander the Great, who overthrew the Persian dynasty ; and for awhile Greece ruled the world. Then came the Cæsars, and founded the empire of Rome—symbolized by the legs of iron—the mightiest power the world had ever known : and for centuries Rome sat on those seven hills, and swayed the sceptre over the nations of the earth. And then, in its turn, the Roman power was broken ; and the mighty empire split up into ten kingdoms corresponding to the ten toes of the prophetic figure.

I believe in the literal fulfilment, so far, of Daniel's God-given words ; and in the sure fulfilment of the final prophecy of the " stone cut out of the mountain, without hands," that by and by shall grind the kingdoms of this world into dust, and bring in the kingdom of peace.

Whilst the feet were of clay, there was some of the strength of the iron remaining in them. At the present day we have got down to the toes, and even to the extremities of these. Soon, very soon, the collision may occur ; and then will come the end. The "stone cut out without hands" is surely coming—and it may be very soon.

What does Ezekiel say, prophesying within some few years of the time of this very vision ?—" Remove the diadem, and take off the crown. . . . . I will overturn, overturn, overturn ; and it shall be no more, until He come whose right it is : and I will give it Him "

What does St. Paul say ?—" The appearing of our Lord Jesus Christ ; which in His time He shall show, who is the blessed and only Potentate ; the King of kings ; and Lord of lords ; . . . . to whom be honour and power everlasting."

Yes, the Fifth Monarchy is coming : and it may be very soon. Hail, thou Fifth Monarch, who art to rule the world in righteousness, and sway the sceptre "from the river unto the ends of the earth." Shortly the cry, " Christ is come ! " will be ringing through the earth. It is only a "little while." Cheer up, ye children of God ; our King will be back by and by ! And to those who have not as yet given their hearts to Christ, I would say, Lose no time ! If you want a part and lot in that coming kingdom of the Lord you had better press into it now while the door is open. By and by "Too late ! too late !" will be the cry.

When King Nebuchadnezzar heard the full description of his dream and listened to its interpretation, he was satisfied that at last he had found a really wise man. He gave Daniel many great gifts, and raised him — just as Pharaoh had raised Joseph ages before — to a place near the throne. And when Daniel was raised to position and power he did not forget his friends ; he requested of the king that they should be promoted ; and they also were put in positions of honour and trust. God blessed them signally ; and—what is more—He kept them true to Him in their prosperity, as they had been in their adversity.

From that moment Daniel becomes a great man. He is set over the province of Babylon : he is lifted right out of bondage ; right out of servitude. He was a young man, probably not more than twenty-two years old : and there he is —set over a mighty empire ; is made, you might say, practically ruler over the whole of the then known world. And God will exalt us when the right time comes. We need not try to promote ourselves ; we need not struggle for position. Let God put us in our true places   And it is a good deal better for a man to be right with God, even if he hold no position down here. Then he can look up and know that God is pleased with him : that is enough.

"FIGHT THE GOOD FIGHT!"

" How goes the fight with thee—
   The life-long battle with all evil things ?
Thine no low strife, and thine no selfish aim ;
   It is the war of giants and of kings.

" Goes the fight well with thee—
   This living fight with death and death's dark power ?
Is not the Stronger than the strong one near,
   With thee and *for* thee in the fiercest hour ?

" Dread not the din and smoke,
   The stifling poison of the fiery air ;
Courage ! it is the battle of thy God :
   Go, and for Him learn how to do and dare !

" What though ten thousand fall,
   And the red field with the dear dead be strewn !
Grasp but more bravely thy bright shield and sword ;
   Fight to the last, although thou fight'st alone.

" What though ten thousand faint,
   Desert, or yield, or in weak terror flee ?
Heed not the panic of the multitude ;
   Thine be the Captain's watchword—VICTORY !"

DR. H. BONAR.

III.

NEBUCHADNEZZAR'S IMAGE.

"Nebuchadnezzar the king made an image of gold, whose height was three-score cubits : he set it up in the plains of Dura in the province of Babylon " (Dan. iii. 1).

TIME went on—possibly several years; and now we reach a crisis indeed. Whether or not that dream of a gigantic human figure continued to haunt Nebuchadnezzar we cannot say; but it is quite possible that the dream may have in some sort suggested Nebuchadnezzar's next proceeding. He ordered the construction of an immense image. It was to be of gold —not simply gilded, but actually of gold. Gold is a symbol of prosperity; and at this time Babylon was prosperous. In like manner in the prosperous days of Jerusalem gold was abundant. And it may have been that some of the precious metal, carried as the spoils of war from the Jewish capital, was used in the construction of this image of gold. It was of colossal size—over ninety feet high, and between nine and ten feet wide. This gigantic image was set up in the plain of Dura, near to the city. I suppose Nebuchadnezzar wanted to gratify his imperial vanity by inaugurating a universal religion.

When the time came for the dedication, Daniel was not

there. He may have been away in Egypt ; or in some one of the many provinces, attending to the affairs of the empire. If he had been there we should have heard of him. Satraps, princes, governors, councillors, high secretaries, judges, were ordered to be present at the dedication of the image. What a gathering that morning ! It was the fashionable thing to be seen that morning driving to the plain of Dura. Of course it was : all the great people, and all the rich people, were to be there. Now hark ! the trumpet sounds ; the herald shouts : " To you it is commanded, O people, nations, and languages, that at what time ye hear the sound of the cornet, flute, harp, sackbut, psaltery, dulcimer, and all kinds of music, ye fall down and worship the golden image that Nebuchadnezzar the king hath set up : and whoso falleth not down and worshippeth, shall the same hour be cast into the midst of a burning fiery furnace."

Perhaps a part of the ceremony consisted in "the unveiling of the statue," as we say. One thing, however, is certain : that at the given signal all the people were required to fall to the earth, and worship.

But in the law of God there was something against that : God's voice had spoken at Sinai ; God's finger had written on the table of stone—"THOU SHALT HAVE NONE OTHER GODS BEFORE ME." God's law went right against the king's. I said Daniel was not on the plain of Dura. But his influence was there. He had influenced those three friends of his—Shadrach, Meshach, and Abednego. They were there ; and they were actuated by the same spirit as Daniel. Their position brought them here at the hour of the dedication.

Now mark you, no man can be true for God, and live for Him, without at some time or other being unpopular in this world. Those men who are trying to live for both worlds make a wreck of it ; for at some time or other the collision is sure to come. Ah, would all of us have advised Daniel's three friends to do the right thing at any hazard? Are there not some of us with so little backbone that we would have counselled these three just to bow down a little, so that no one could take notice—to merely bow down, but not to worship? Daniel and his friends, when they first came to Babylon, perceived that the two worlds—the present world and the world to come—would be in collision: and they "went for" the world to come; they "went for" things unseen: they did not judge for the time being only; they took their stand right there. Even if it cost them their lives, what of that! It would only hasten them to the glory; and they would receive the greater reward. They took their stand for God and for the unseen world. The faithful three utterly refused to bend the knee to a god of gold.

A terrible penalty was associated with disobedience to the king's command: "Whoso falleth not down and worshippeth shall the same hour be cast into the midst of a burning fiery furnace."*

How many would cry out in this city—in every city—"Give me gold, give me money; and I will do anything." Some people may think and say that the men of Nebuchadnezzar's day ought not to have bowed down to a golden idol; but they themselves are every day doing just that very thing. Money is their god; social position their golden image. There are plenty of men to-day who are bowing down to the golden image that the world has set up. "Give me gold! give me gold; and you

---

* Not a mere empty threat. It was a sentence in harmony with the character and the practice of the ferocious and cruel king. "The Lord make them like Zedekiah and like Ahab, whom the King of Babylon ROASTED IN THE FIRE" (Jer. xxix. 22).

It is well for us to remember that the burning of living beings has not been confined to a distant country and a barbarous age. Some three hundred years ago, an English queen, whose name has become a proverb, caused to be roasted alive in England, during her short reign of five years and five months, no less than 277 persons; *of whom fifty-five were women, and four were children.*

may have heaven. Give me position; and you may have the world to come. Give me worldly honour; and I will sell out my hopes of heaven. Give me the thirty pieces of silver; and I will give you Christ." That is the cry of the world to-day.

And now the order is given—very probably by the king himself—that the bands should strike up; just the same as on public occasions bands of music do now. The music could be heard afar off; and when the first notes burst forth all were to bow down to the golden image. Earth's great ones and mighty ones bowed down at the king's command. But there were three with stiff knees which did not bend. Those were Daniel's three friends, who knew well that to do the king's bidding would be to break the law of their God; and they at all events will not fall down and worship. At the king's command they had come to the dedication: there might be nothing wrong in that: but they will not bow down. They were too stiff in the backbone for that. They remembered the command, "Thou shalt have none other gods before Me." These are the kind of servants God wants—men who will stand up bravely and fearlessly for Him.

Like all the servants of the Lord, and all who walk in the atmosphere of heaven, these three Hebrews had enemies. There were some who bore them a bitter grudge. Very possibly they were thought to have had undue preference in being promoted to office. So there were some others, besides the three young Hebrews, who did not worship as commanded. Do you know what they were doing? They were watching to see Shadrach, Meshach, and Abednego. If they themselves had bowed their faces to the ground, according to Nebuchadnezzar's command, they would not have seen that Daniel's three friends refused to bow: they would not have seen the three young Hebrews standing up, erect, straight. There were those Chaldæans looking out of the corners of their eyes, and watching the three young men. These young Jews had so carried themselves, and had so lived in Babylon, that their watchers felt sure they would not bow down. They knew well that the three would not sacrifice principle. They would go as far as it was lawful in obeying the king's commands; but a time would come when they would draw the line. When the commands of the earthly sovereign come in conflict with the commands of the God of heaven they will not yield. The watchers watched; but the young men did not bow.

Thank God, they had backbone, if you will allow me the expression. Something held their knees firm; they would not give in: there they stood as firm as rock. They did not get half-way down, and just make believe that they were going to worship the image : there was nothing of that kind: they stood up erect and firm.

Some of those Chaldæans wished to get rid of these young Hebrews : they perhaps wanted their places : they were after their offices. Men have been the same in all ages. There were, no doubt, a good many men in Babylon who wanted to get their posts. These three men had high positions; there was a good deal of honour attached to their offices : and their enemies wanted to oust them, and to succeed to their offices. It is a very bad state of things when men try to pull down others in order to obtain their places ; and there is a good deal of that, you know, in this world. Many a man has had his character blasted and ruined by some person or other who wanted to step into his place and position.

So away went those men to the king to lay an information. They duly rendered the salutation, "O king, live for ever!" and then they went on to tell him of those rebellious Hebrews who would not obey the king's order. " Do you know, O king, that there are three men in your kingdom who will not obey your command ?"

" Three men in my kingdom who will not obey me ! " roars Nebuchadnezzar; " no ! who are they? what are their names ? "

" Why, those three Hebrew slaves whom you set over us—Shadrach, Meshach, and Abednego. When the music struck up they did not bow down; and it is noised all around : the people know it. And if you allow them to go unpunished, it will not be long before your law will be perfectly worthless."

I can imagine the king almost speechless with rage, and just gesturing his commands that the men should be brought before him.

" Is it true, O Shadrach, Meshach, and Abednego, that you would not bow down and worship the golden image which I set up in the plain of Dura ? "

" It is true, quite true," says one of them—perhaps Shadrach. " Quite true, O king."

One last chance Nebuchadnezzar resolved to give them. " Now, if ye be ready that at what time ye hear the sound of the cornet, flute, harp, sackbut, psaltery, and dulcimer, and all kinds of music, ye fall down and worship the image which I have made—well : but if ye worship not, ye shall be cast the same hour into the midst of a burning fiery furnace. And who is that God that shall deliver you out of my hands ? "

That is pretty plain speaking, is it not? There is no mincing or smoothing over matters. Do this, and live ; do not do it, and you die. But the threat that the king held out had few terrors for them. They turned and said to the king : " O Nebuchadnezzar, we are not careful to answer thee in this matter. If it be so, our God whom we serve is able to deliver us from the burning fiery furnace ; and He will deliver us out of thine hand, O king. But if not, be it known unto thee, O king, that we will not serve thy gods, nor worship the golden image which thou hast set up."

And that is plain speaking, too. The king of Babylon

had not been accustomed to be talked to like that. And he did not like it. We are told he was " full of fury."

These Hebrews spoke respectfully, but firmly. And mark, they did not absolutely say that God *would* deliver them from the burning fiery furnace; but they declared that He was *able* to deliver them. They had no doubt about His ability to do it. They believed that He would do it; but they did not hide from themselves the possibility of Nebuchadnezzar being allowed to carry out his threats. Still, that did not greatly move them. " But *if not* "—if in His inscrutable purposes He allows us to suffer—still our resolve is the same : " we will not serve thy gods, nor worship the golden image which thou hast set up." They were not afraid to pass from the presence of the king of Babylon to the presence of the King of kings. They had courage, those men. I wonder if there could be found three such brave men in New York, or in Boston, or in Baltimore, or in Chicago, now. How settled they were in their minds ! Thank God for such courage ! thank God for such boldness ! A few such men, brave and fearless for God, would soon turn the world upside down. Nowadays they would be thought fanatics : they would be advised to bow down outwardly, and never to mind the " worship " of the image. But even the semblance of worshipping an image was too much for them ; and they were determined to avoid even the appearance of evil.

Look at the king ! I can imagine him in his fury, trembling like an aspen leaf, and turning pale as death with rage. " What ! disobey me, the great and mighty king? Call in the mighty men ; and let them bind these rebels hand and foot. Heat the furnace seven times hotter than its wont; and then in with these rebellious fellows ! They shall not live."

" Then these men were bound in their coats, their hosen, and their hats, and their other garments, and were cast into the midst of the burning fiery furnace."

The command was instantly executed; and they were hurled into the terrible blaze. The fire was so furious that the flames consumed the officers who thrust them in.* The three young Hebrews "fell down bound into the midst of the burning fiery furnace;" and it seemed as if they were in a bad case then. From his royal seat the king peered forth, looking out to see the rebels burnt to ashes. But when Nebuchadnezzar gazed, expecting the gratification of his vengeance, to his great amazement he saw the men walking about in the midst of the flames; walking, mind you—they were not running—walking as if in the midst of green pastures or on the margin of still waters. There was no difference in them, except that their bonds were burnt off. Ah, it does my heart good to think that the worst the devil is allowed to do is to burn off the bonds of God's children. If Christ be with us, the direst afflictions can only loosen our earthly bonds, and set us free to soar the higher.

Nebuchadnezzar beheld strange things that day. There, through the flames, he saw FOUR men walking in the midst of the fire, although only three had been cast therein. How was this? The Great Shepherd in yonder heaven saw that three of His lambs were in trouble; and He leaped down from there right into the fiery furnace. And when Nebuchadnezzar looked in, a fourth form was to be seen.

"Did not we cast three men bound into the midst of the fire? They answered and said unto the king, True, O king.

---

* Those who have stood upon the "feed" platform of a great iron-smelting furnace, and have felt the enormous pressure of the atmosphere as it rushes forward to fill up the vacuum caused by the rarefaction of the air from the furnace, and have experienced the *suck* or *draw* towards the edge of the platform which is felt when the furnace doors are thrown open, will easily understand how perilous a near approach to the mouth would be likely to prove; and how easily Nebuchadnezzar's "mighty men" would themselves be drawn into the power of the flames, if they once ventured within the range of their attraction.

He answered and said, Lo, I see four men loose, walking in the midst of the fire, and they have no hurt; and the form of the fourth is like the Son of God."

It was doubtless the Son of God.* That Great Shepherd of the sheep saw that three of His true servants were in peril; and He came from His Father's presence and His Father's bosom to be with them in it. There had been One watching that terrible scene of attempting to burn the faithful; and His tender pitying eye saw that men were condemned to death because of their loyalty to Him. With one great leap He sprang from the Father's presence, from His palace in glory, right down into the fiery furnace, and was by their side before the heat of the fire could come near unto them. Jesus was with His servants as the flames wreathed around them. And not a hair of their heads was singed; they were not scorched; not even the smell of fire was upon them I can almost fancy I hear them chanting: "When thou passest through the waters I will be with thee; and through the rivers, they shall not overflow thee; *when thou walkest through the fire, thou shalt not be burned; neither shall the flame kindle upon thee."*

God can take care of us when we pass through the waters; God can take care of us when we pass through the fires. God is able to take care of us, if we will but stand up for Him: God will take care of us, if we will but stand up for Him. Young man, honour God; and God will honour you. What you have to do is to take your stand upon God's side. And if you have to go against the whole world, take that stand. Dare to do right; dare to be true; dare to be honest: let the consequences be what they may. You may have to forfeit your situation; because you cannot, and will

---

* That the fourth was the Lord Jesus Christ—He who appeared to Abraham, and who wrestled with Jacob—has been an accepted truth with almost every one who ministers the word. It is only fair to say that in the original the definite article is absent; and the sentence reads, "like a son of gods."

not, do something which your employer requires you to
do, but which your conscience tells you is wrong.   Give
up your situation then, rather than give up your principles
If your employer requires you to sell goods by means
of misrepresentation, fraud, or falsehood, give up your
situation, and say, "I will rather die a pauper; I will rather
die in a poorhouse; than be unfaithful to my principles." That
is the kind of stuff those men were made of.   These glorious
heroes braved even death because God was with them.   O
friends, we want to be Christians with the same backbone:
men and women who are prepared to stand up for the right,
heeding not what the world may say or what the world may
think.

"Then Nebuchadnezzar came near to the mouth of the
burning fiery furnace, and spake, and said, Shadrach,
Meshach, and Abednego, ye servants of the Most High
God, come forth, and come hither."   And they walked
out, untouched by the fire.   They came out, like
giants in their conscious strength.   I can fancy how the
princes, the governors, the counsellors, and the great men,
crowded around them to see such an unheard-of sight.
Their garments showed no trace of fire; their hair even was
not singed—as if God would teach that He guards even
"the very hairs of our head."   Nebuchadnezzar had defied
God; and had been conquered.   God had proved Himself
"able" to deliver His servants out of the king's hand.
Nebuchadnezzar accepted his defeat.   And he makes a
decree: "That every people, nation, and language, which
speak anything against the God of Shadrach, Meshach, and
Abednego, shall be cut in pieces, and their houses shall be
made a dunghill: because there is no other God that can
deliver after this sort."

And he promoted these three witnesses to higher place
and position, and put greater honour upon them.   God stood

by them because they had stood by Him. He will have us learn to do a thing just because it is right, and not because it is popular. The outlook may appear like death : but do the right ; and, if we stand firm, God will bring everything for the best.

That is the last we hear of these three men. God sent them to Babylon to shine   and they shone.

"LIVING ! WORKING ! WAITING !"

" Who would not *live* for Jesus,
   Rejoicing, glad and free ?
The music of a ransomed life
   Is all He asks from thee.

" Who would not *work* for Jesus,
   When service is but song ?—
The rippling of a stream of love
   That bears thy soul along ?

" Who would not *die* for Jesus,
   When death is victory ?—
The grand, o'ershadowing portal-gate
   Guarding eternity ?

" Who would not *wait* for Jesus,
   And waiting, sweetly sing?
Hushing their heart with promises
While tarrying for their King ? "

EVA TRAVERS POOLE.

IV.

NEBUCHADNEZZAR'S SECOND DREAM.

"I, Nebuchadnezzar, was at rest in mine house, and flourishing in my palace: I saw a dream which made me afraid, and the thoughts upon my bed and the visions of my head troubled me" (Dan. iv. 5).

Y AND BY Nebuchadnezzar had another dream. Surely this man will be brought to see God's hand at last. How many signs and wonders has he seen, fitted to convince him of God's mighty power! This time he remembers the particulars of the dream well enough: they stand out vivid and clear to his mind. Again he calls in the four classes of men on whom he counts to make dark things light, and hidden things plain; and he recounts to them the incidents of this dream. But the magicians, the astrologers, the Chaldæans, and the soothsayers, are all at fault: they cannot tell him the interpretation. When called upon to interpret his former dream they all stood silent. And they stood silent again as the second dream is unfolded to them. There was something in these dreams of the king which stopped their mouths—usually so ready with some plausible interpretation. With these royal dreams it was no use: they were beaten.

It would appear that Nebuchadnezzar had half-forgotten the man who had recounted to him his former dream, and given its interpretation. He says, "At last Daniel came before me." And he proceeds to address Daniel by his Chaldæan name of Belteshazzar. "O Belteshazzar, master of the

magicians, because I know that the spirit of the holy gods is
in thee, and no secret troubleth thee, tell me the visions of my
dream that I have seen, and the interpretation thereof. Thus
were the visions of mine head in my bed; I saw, and behold
a tree in the midst of the earth, and the height thereof was
great. The tree grew, and was strong; and the height thereof
reached unto heaven, and the sight thereof to the end of all the
earth: the leaves thereof were fair and the fruit thereof much,
and in it was meat for all: the beasts of the field had shadow
under it, and the fowls of the heaven dwelt in the boughs
thereof, and all flesh was fed of it. I saw in the visions of my
head upon my bed; and behold, a watcher and an holy one
came down from heaven: he cried aloud, and said thus, Hew
down the tree and cut off his branches, shake off his leaves,
and scatter his fruit: let the beasts get away from under it, and
the fowls from his branches: nevertheless leave the stump of
his roots in the earth, even with a band of iron and brass, in
the tender grass of the field; and let it be wet with the dew of
heaven, and let his portion be with the beasts in the grass of
the earth: let his heart be changed from man's, and let a
beast's heart be given unto him; and let seven times pass over
him. This matter is by the decree of the watchers, and the
demand by the word of the holy ones: to the intent that the
living may know that the Most High ruleth in the kingdom of
men, and giveth it to whomsoever He will, and setteth up over
it the basest of men. This dream I, King Nebuchadnezzar,
have seen. Now thou, O Belteshazzar, declare the interpretation thereof, forasmuch as all the wise men of my kingdom
are not able to make known unto me the interpretation: but
thou art able: for the spirit of the holy gods is in thee."

As soon as the prophet appears upon the scene the king
feels sure that he will now get the meaning of the dream.

For a time Daniel stands still and motionless. Does his
heart fail him? The record simply says he " was astonied for

one hour; and his thoughts troubled him." He saw what
was meant by the royal dream—that the king was to have
a terrible fall; and that the kingdom was, at least for a
season, to be taken from this proud monarch. The ready
words rush to his lips; but he hates to let them out. He
does not want to tell Nebuchadnezzar that his kingdom and
his mind are both about to depart from him; and that he is
to wander forth to eat grass like a beast. The king, too,
hesitates : a dark foreboding for a time gets the better of his
curiosity. But soon he nerves himself to hear the worst; and
in kindly words desires Daniel to proceed, to tell out all he
knows. And Daniel breaks the silence. He does not smooth
over the matter; but speaks out plainly. There and then he
preached righteousness to the king. A very good sermon it
was too that he preached. If we had more of the same sort
now it would be the better for us. He entreats the king to
" break off his sins by righteousness, and his iniquities by
showing mercy to the poor : if it may be a lengthening of thy
tranquillity."

Perhaps he told him, for his encouragement, how the
King of Nineveh, more than two centuries before, had repented
at the preaching of Jonah. He unfolds the full meaning of the
dream. He tells the king that the great and strong tree
symbolizes Nebuchadnezzar himself; and that just as the tree
was hewn down and destroyed, so will he himself be shorn of
power and robbed of strength. Daniel tells him that he will
be driven from among men, and have to herd with the beasts
of the field : yet that nevertheless the kingdom should in the
end revert to him, just as the great watcher had spared the
stump of the tree.

Repentance might have deferred, or even averted, the threat-
ened calamity. But at that time he "repented not." And twelve
months afterwards the king. heedless of the prophetic warning,
and lifted up with pride, walked either through the corridors

of his great palace, or out upon its roof; looked forth upon the city's vast extent; gazed at those hanging gardens which counted as one of the wonders of the world; and said: "Is not this great Babylon, that I have built for the house of the kingdom, by the might of my power, and for the honour of my majesty?"

A voice from heaven instantly cried, "The kingdom is departed from thee." And then and there God touched his reason: it reeled and tottered on its throne, and fled. He was driven forth from men; he herded with animals; his body was wet with the dew of heaven. This greatest of princes had gone clean mad. It would not take me fifteen minutes to-day to prove that the world has gone clean mad; and the mass of professing Christians too. Do not men think and talk as if everything were done by their own power? Is not God completely forgotten? Do not men neglect every warning that He in mercy sends? Yes, men are mad, and nothing short of it.

NEBUCHADNEZZAR'S REPENTANCE.

But Nebuchadnezzar's kingdom had not passed away from him irrevocably; for, according to the prophet's word, at the close of the " seven times " his understanding returned to him; he resumed his throne and his authority; and his counsellors and officers again gathered around him. His power has been given back to him; and he is now a very different man. Of a truth the king's reason has returned to him; and he is possessed of a very different spirit. He sends forth a new proclamation giving honour to the Most High, and extolling the God of heaven. Its closing words show his repentance, and tend to prove that Daniel had brought this mighty king to God.

It is interesting to go over the different proclamations of Nebuchadnezzar, and note the change that takes place in them. He sent out one proclamation setting forth what other people ought to do, and how they should serve the God of these Hebrews. But the truth did not get home to himself until now. Here is his closing proclamation: "At the end of the days, I, Nebuchadnezzar, lifted up mine eyes unto heaven, and mine understanding returned unto me; and I blessed the Most High, and I praised and honoured Him that liveth for ever, whose dominion is an everlasting dominion, and His kingdom is from generation to generation. At the same time my reason returned unto me : and for the glory of my kingdom, mine honour and brightness returned unto me ; and my counsellors, and my lords sought unto me : and I was established in my kingdom, and excellent majesty was added unto me. Now I, Nebuchadnezzar, praise and extol and honour the King of heaven, all whose works are truth, and His ways judgment : and those that walk in pride He is able to abase."

When you find that a man has got to praising God it is a good sign. The earlier edict said much about other people's duty towards the God of the Hebrews, but nothing about what the king himself should do. Oh, let us get to personal love, personal praise ! That is what is wanted in the church in the present day. Nebuchadnezzar passes from the stage : this is the last record we have of him. But we may surely hope that, like that of the Corinthians, his was a "repentance to salvation not to be repented of." And if this were so we may well believe that to-day Nebuchadnezzar the king and Daniel the captive are walking the crystal pavement of heaven arm-in-arm together; and, it may be, talking over the old times in Babylon. Now, if the young prophet had been of a vacillating character ; if he had been of a willowy growth, liable to be shaken by every wind, and had not stood there in that city like a great oak—do you think he would have won this mighty monarch to his religion and his God ? As a result of that young man going to that heathen city and standing firm for his God, and the God of the Bible, the Lord honoured him, and gave him that mighty monarch as a star in his crown. We may fairly say that King Nebuchadnezzar was led to the God of the Hebrews through the faith of this Hebrew's love—just because he had

> "a purpose firm,
> And dared to make it known."

THE MASTER'S SERVICE.

"Service of Jesus! Oh, service of sweetness!
   There are no bonds in that service for me;
Full of delight and most perfect completeness:
   Evermore His, yet so joyously free!

"Service of Jesus! Oh, service of power!
   Sharing His glory, while sharing His shame!
All the best blessings the Master can shower
   Rest on the servant exalting His name.

"Service of Jesus! Oh, service joy-giving!
   Melting our hearts into rivers of love;
Secret of life and the sweetness of living,
   Joy felt on earth that will fill us above.

"Service of Jesus! Oh, service of praising!
   Such as redeemed ones rejoicing can sing,
Daily and hourly their voices upraising,
   Lauding their Saviour, extolling their King."

EVA TRAVERS POOLE.

V.

THE HANDWRITING ON THE WALL.

" Belshazzar the king made a great feast to a thousand of his lords, and drank wine before the thousand " (Dan. v. 1).

AND now, for twenty long years or more, we lose sight of Daniel. He may possibly have been for a portion of the interval living in retirement; but at the end of it he still appears to be holding some appointment at the Babylonish court; although most likely occupying a less prominent position than of yore. Nebuchadnezzar had died; and there was now ruling in Babylon, or it may be acting in some such position as "Regent," a young man whose name was Belshazzar.* This youthful ruler "made a great feast to a thousand of his lords,

---

* It is thought by scholars that Belshazzar was admitted to a share of the sovereignty in conjunction with his father Nabonadius, in much the same way as, years previously, Nebuchadnezzar had reigned in association with his father. It has been further stated that Nabonadius had shortly before fought a battle with Cyrus, been worsted, and had taken refuge in Borsippa. Consequently, Belshazzar was acting in his father's stead. But what a time for revelry, with a victorious enemy at the gates, and a father shut up in a beleaguered fortress! The siege of Paris going on at the same time as the investment of Metz, presents something like a modern parallel to the position of affairs.

Reverting for a moment to Nebuchadnezzar, the fact that for a time he shared in his father's kingly authority, before becoming sole sovereign, explains some apparent difficulty as to dates. For example, Nebuchadnezzar is termed " King of Babylon," when he first lays siege to Jerusalem (Dan. i. 1; 2 Kings xxiv. 1; 2 Chron. xxxvi. 6). He carries away Daniel and other captives as

and drank wine before the thousand." Of this prince we only get a single glimpse. This scene of the feast is the first and last view we have of him ; and it is enough. How long that banqueting lasted we do not know; but in the East feasts often extend over many days. Amongst the Jews seven days was not an unusual time for the duration of a feast, and occasionally the time was extended to twice seven days, *i.e.*, four-teen days. It was a "great feast." The king caroused with his satraps and princes, his lords, and the mighty men of Babylon, together with his wives and concubines, drinking and rioting, and praising the "gods of gold, and of silver, of brass, of iron, of wood, and of stone." That is pretty much what men are doing to-day, if they are bowing their knee to the god of this world. Cyrus, the great Persian general, is outside the gates, besieging the city, just as Nebuchadnezzar had besieged Jerusalem. And this Belshazzar fancies himself secure behind the lofty and massive walls that encompass Babylon.

The revellers wax daring and wanton. They had forgotten the power of the God of the Hebrews, as shown in the days of Nebuchadnezzar. Heated with wine and lifted up with pride, they laid their sacrilegious hands on the golden

hostages, and returns to Babylon. He then commands that the education and training of the four young Hebrews is to be effected, and allots *three years* for the purpose. Three years are passed in their instruction ; and they are then admitted into the order of the magi, or wise men. (Compare Dan. i. 5 ; i. 18; ii. 13.) And yet, although between three and four years have elapsed since the siege of Jerusalem, Nebuchadnezzar's dream is said to have occurred in the " second year" of his reign. There is a seeming discrepancy here. But let it be understood that the term "second year" in Dan. ii. 1, refers to the time subsequent to his father's death, during which he had reigned alone ; and the difficulty is removed.

The instance of the " regency" in England, during which period the Prince Regent acted with large powers, "in all but name a king," although George III. still lived, will serve partially to illustrate the position of Nebuchadnezzar at one time, and of Belshazzar at another ; although the parallel is by no means complete.

vessels which had been brought out of the temple of the house of God which was at Jerusalem; and out of those sacred cups they drank. And as they drank to their idols, one can readily believe that they scoffed at the God of Israel. I could almost picture the scene before me now, and can imagine I hear them blaspheming His holy name. Now they make merry; now they are in the midst of their boisterous revelry. But lo! stop! What is the matter? The king is struck by something that he sees! His countenance has changed. He has turned deadly pale! The wine cup has fallen from his grasp! His knees smite together. He trembles from head to foot. I should not wonder if his lords and nobles did not laugh in their sleeve at him, thinking he was drunk. But, there, along the wall, standing out in living light, are seen letters of strange and unintelligible shape. "In the same hour came forth fingers of a man's hand, and wrote over against the candlestick upon the plaster of the wall of the king's palace; and the king saw the part of the hand that wrote."

Above the golden candlestick,* on a bare space of the wall,† Belshazzar beholds that mysterious handwriting. He distinctly discerns the tracing of those terrible words. Was that writing on the palace wall the work of the same hand that had traced the tables of stone at Sinai? Or did some angel-

---

* A recent writer says: "The fingers 'wrote over against the candlestick." What candlestick? 'The candlestick of gold, with the lamps thereof,' which Solomon had made. It was there exhibited in mockery and triumph; as, ages after, its counterpart adorned the triumph of the Roman emperor, and was sculptured in bas-relief on the Arch of Titus, to be seen in Rome this very day."—DANIEL: STATESMAN AND PROPHET, Page 160.

† The writing was traced on the plain plaster on the walls of the banquet-room; such as, notwithstanding the then prevailing taste for ornament, is still found on the palaces of Nineveh. Those who have seen Mr. Layard's large and magnificent drawings of Assyrian antiquities, will remember that elaborate decoration extends only to a certain height. Above that line the wall is quite plain, and is, to this day, coated with lime."—DANIEL: STATESMAN AND PROPHET, Page 160.

messenger execute the Divine commission? The words, "fingers of a man's hand," seem to imply the latter.

The king cries aloud, and commands that the astrologers, the Chaldæans, and the soothsayers, should be brought forward. They come trooping in ; and he says to them : " Whosoever shall read this writing, and show me the interpretation thereof, shall be clothed with scarlet (or purple), and have a chain of gold about his neck, and shall be the third ruler* in the kingdom."

One after another tries to spell out that writing; but they fail to understand it. They are skilled in Chaldæan learning ; but this inscription baffles them. They cannot make out the meaning, any more than an unrenewed man can make out the Bible. They do not understand God's writing: they cannot comprehend it. A man must be born of the Spirit before he can understand God's Book or God's writing. No uncircumcised eyes could decipher those words of fire.

The queen † hears of the state of affairs, and comes in to encourage and advise. She salutes the king with the words, "O king, live for ever ! let not thy thoughts trouble thee, nor let thy countenance be changed " ; and then she goes on to tell him that there is one man in the kingdom who will be able to read the writing, and tell out its meaning. She proceeds to say that in the days of Nebuchadnezzar, " light, and understanding, and wisdom, like the wisdom of the gods, was found in him " ; and advises that Daniel shall be summoned.

For some—perhaps several—years he may have been comparatively little known : may have " dropped out of notice," as we say. But now, for the third time, he stands before a Babylonian ruler to interpret and to reveal, when the powers

* " The third ruler," mark that ! Belshazzar's father, Nabonadius, probably counting as the *first ;* Belshazzar, the associate-king, as the *second ;* and the successful interpreter, as the *third.*

† From the authority with which she speaks, it has been conjectured that this was the queen-mother.

of its magicians and astrologers have utterly failed. Daniel comes in; and his eye lights up as he sees the letters upon the wall. He can read the meaning of the words. The king puts forth his offer of rewards; but Daniel is unmoved: "Let thy gifts be to thyself, and give thy rewards to another: yet I will read the writing unto the king, and make known to him the interpretation."

But before he reads the words upon the wall he gives the king a bit of his mind. Perhaps he had been long praying for an opportunity of warning him; and now he has it, he will not let it slip, although all those mighty lords are there. So he reminds the king of the lessons he ought to have learned from the visitation that fell upon the mighty Nebuchadnezzar: of how that monarch had been humbled, brought down, and deposed from his kingly throne, because " his heart was lifted up, and his mind hardened in pride ;" until at length he came to repentance, and realized that the Most High God ruleth in the kingdom of men. "And thou his son,* O Belshazzar, hast not humbled thine heart, though thou knewest all this; but hast lifted up thyself against the Lord of heaven."

Then looking up at the mystic words standing forth in their lambent light, he reads:

" MENE, MENE, TEKEL, UPHARSIN:"

MENE: God hath numbered thy kingdom, and finished it.

TEKEL: Thou art weighed in the balances, and art found wanting.

UPHARSIN:† Thy kingdom is divided, and given to the Medes and Persians.

---

* Here, as in several other instances, " son " is used for " grandson " ; and " father " is used for " grandfather."

† In interpreting, Daniel reads PERES, which is the singular form of the word of which PHARSIN is the plural. The U is the prefixed conjunction " and." (See " DANIEL : STATESMAN AND PROPHET," pp. 171—2.)

How the word of doom must have rung through the palace that night! There was an awful warning. Sinner, it is for you. What if God should put you in the balance, and you without Christ! What would become of your soul? Take warning by Belshazzar's fate.

The destruction did not tarry. The king thought he was perfectly secure: he considered that the walls of Babylon were impregnable. But "in that night," at the very hour when Daniel was declaring the doom of the king, Cyrus, the conquering Persian, was turning the Euphrates from its regular course and channel, and was bringing his army within those gigantic walls: the guard around the palace is beaten back; the Persian soldiers force their way to the banqueting-hall; and Belshazzar's blood flows mingling with the outpoured wine upon the palace floor.

It was Belshazzar's last night. One short chapter gives us all we know of that young monarch. His life was short. The wicked do not live out half their days. An impious young man, he had neglected or forgotten the holy Daniel: he had set aside his father's counsellor and friend: he had turned away from the best adviser and most faithful servant that Nebuchadnezzar had ever had—one who probably had done more than any one else to build up and consolidate his kingdom. And this is his end.

O sinners, take warning: Death and hell are right upon you—death and hell, I say. And they are just as close, it may be, as was the sword of the slayer to those midnight revellers.

VI.

THE EDICT OF DARIUS.

"To establish a royal statute, and to make a firm decree, that whosoever shall ask a petition of any god or man for thirty days, save of thee, O king, he shall be cast into the den of lions." (Dan. vi. 7.)

E find that Darius—who was probably one of the high military commanders engaged in the siege of Babylon—takes the kingdom, while Cyrus is off conquering other parts of the world. As soon as he attains the throne he makes his arrangements for governing the country. He divides the kingdom into one hundred and twenty provinces; and he appoints a prince or ruler over each province; and over the princes he puts three presidents to see that these rulers do no damage to the king, and do not swindle the government. And over these three he places Daniel, as president of the presidents. Very possibly Darius knew the man. He may have been in former days at the court of Nebuchadnezzar; and if so, he probably considered Daniel an able and conscientious statesman. Anyhow, the king either knew, or was told, sufficient to justify his confidence. And now Daniel is again in office. He held in that day the highest position, under the sovereign, that any one could hold. He was next to the throne. If you will allow me the expression, he was the Bismarck or the Gladstone of the empire. He was Prime Minister; he was Secretary of State; and all important matters would pass through his hands.

We do not know how long he held that position. But sooner or late the other presidents and the princes grew jealous, and wanted Daniel out of the way. It was as if they had said, "Let us see if we cannot get this sanctimonious Hebrew removed: he has 'bossed' us long enough." You see he was so impracticable: they could do nothing with him. There were plenty of collectors and treasurers; but he kept such a close eye on them that they only made their salaries. There was no chance of plundering the government while he was at the head. He was president, and probably all the revenue accounts passed before him. No doubt these enemies wanted to form a "ring." And they may have talked somewhat after this fashion: "If it were not for this man we could form a 'ring'; and then, in three or four years, we could make enough to enable us to retire from office, and have a villa on the banks of the Euphrates; or we could go down to Egypt, and see something of the world. We could have plenty of money—all we should ever want, or our children either—if we could only just get control of the government, and manage things as we should like to. As things go now we only just get our exact dues; and it will take years and years for them to mount up to anything respectable. If we had matters in our own hands it would be different; for King Darius does not know half as much about the affairs of this empire as does this old Hebrew: and he watches our accounts so closely that we can get no advantage over the Government. Down with this pious Jew!"

Perhaps they worked matters so as to get an investigating committee, hoping to catch him in his accounts. But it was no use. If he had put any relatives in office unfairly it would have been found out. And if he had been guilty of peculation, or in any way broken the unalterable laws of the kingdom, the matter would have come to light.

Now I want to call your attention to the fact that one of the highest eulogies ever paid to a man on earth was pronounced

upon Daniel at this time by his enemies. These men were connected with the various parts of the kingdom, and on laying
their heads together they came to this conclusion—that they
could " find no occasion against this Daniel, except they found
it against him concerning the law of his God." What a
testimony from his bitterest enemies ! Would that it could be
said of all of us ! He had never taken a bribe : he had never
been connected with a "ring" : he had never planted a friend
into some fat office with the design of sharing the plunder and
enriching himself. If he had been guilty in any of these things
these scrutineers would have found it out : they had a keen
scent : they were sharp men : they knew all about his actions
and his history : and they would have been glad to have found
out something — anything — which would have led to his
removal from his high position. But they said—and said
with regret : " We shall not find any occasion against him."
Ah, how his name shines ! He had commenced to shine in his
early manhood ; and he shone right along. Now he is an old
man, an old statesman ; and yet this is their testimony. There
had been no sacrifice of principle in order to catch votes ; no
buying up of men's votes or men's consciences ; no " counting
in " or " counting out." There had been none of that. He
had walked right straight along.

Young man, character is worth more than money. Character is worth more than anything else in the wide world.
I would rather in my old age have such a character as that
which Daniel's enemies gave him than have raised over my dead
body a monument of gold reaching from earth to sky. I would
rather have such a testimony as that borne of Daniel than have
all that this world can give.

The men said, " We will get him out of the way. We
will get the king to sign a decree; and we will propose a
penalty. It shall not be the fiery furnace this time. We
will have a lions' den—a den of angry lions ; and they will

soon make away with him." Probably these plotters met
at night, for it generally happens that if men want to do
any downright mean business they meet at night : darkness
suits them best. The chief-president himself was not there :
he had not been invited to meet them. Very likely some
lawyer, who understood all about the laws of the Medes and
Persians, stood up, and talked something after this fashion:
"Gentlemen, I have got, I think, a plan that will work well,
by which we may get rid of this old Hebrew. You know he
will not serve any but the God of Abraham and of Isaac."

We know that very well. And if a man had gone to Babylon
in those days he would not have had to ask if Daniel loved the
God of the Bible. I pity any man who lives so that people
have to ask, "Is he a Christian?" Let us so live that no one
need ask that question about us. These men knew very well
that Daniel worshipped none other than the God of the Bible,
the God of the Hebrews, the God of Abraham, and the God
of Moses ; the God who had brought His people Israel out of
Egypt, through the Red Sea, and into the Promised Land :
they knew that very well.

And these plotters said one to another, "Now, let us get
Darius to sign a decree that if any man make a request of
any God or man— except of the King Darius—for thirty
days, he shall be put into the lions' den. And let us all
keep perfectly still about this matter, so that it won't get
out. We must not tell our wives, for fear the news may get
about the city : Daniel would find it all out ; and he has more
influence with the king than all the rest of us put together.
The king would never sign the decree if he found out what the
object was." Then they may have said, " We must draw it so
tight that Darius will not be able to get out of it after he has
once signed. We must make it so binding that if the king
once signs we shall have that Daniel in the lions' den : and we
will take good care that the lions shall be hungry."

When the mine is all ready, the conspirators come to the king, and open their business with flattering speech : " King Darius, live for ever ! " When people approach me with smooth and oily words, I know they have something else coming – I know they have some purpose in telling me I am a good man. These plotters, perhaps, go on to tell the king how prosperous the realm is, and how much the people think of him. And then, perhaps, in the most plausible way, they tell him that if he signs this decree he will be remembered by their children's children—that it would be a memorial for ever of his greatness and goodness. " What is this decree that you wish me to sign ? " And running his eye over the document he says, " I don't see any objection to that." " Will you put your signet to it, and make it law ? " He puts his signature to the decree, and seals it with his seal. And one of them says, " The law of the Medes and Persians, which altereth not ? " and the king answers, " Oh, yes ; the law of the Medes and Persians : that is it." In the pleasure of granting the request of these people he thinks nothing about Daniel ; and the presidents and princes carefully refrain from jogging his memory. They had told the king a lie, too ; for they said, " ALL the presidents of the kingdom, the governors, and the princes, the counsellors, and the captains, have consulted together to establish a royal statute " ; although the chief-president knew nothing at all about it.

There was probably a long preamble, telling him how popular he was ; saying that he was liked better than Nebuchadnezzar or Belshazzar. They most likely tickled his vanity, and told him that he was the most popular man that had ever reigned in Babylon ; and then they may have gone on to tell him how attached they were to him and his rule, and that they had been consulting together what they could do to increase his popularity and make him more beloved ; and now they had hit upon a plan that was almost sure to do it. They would point out that if no one called upon any god for thirty days, but only on him, the king, making him a god, it would render him the most popular monarch that had ever reigned in Babylonia ; and his name would be handed down to posterity.   And if he could get men to call upon his name for thirty days they would probably keep it up, and so permanently reckon him among the gods.

If you touch a man's vanity he will do almost anything ; and Darius was like most of the human race.   They touched his vanity by intimating that this would make him great.   He thought it a very wise suggestion, and he agreed with them exactly.

It was not only Daniel they were thus going to get out of the way, but every conscientious Jew.   There was not a true Jew in the whole of that wide empire who would bow down and worship Darius ; and these men knew that : and so they were going to sweep away at a stroke all the Jews who were true to their faith.   They hated them.

And I want to tell you that the world does not love Christians nowadays.   The world will persecute a man if he attempts to live the life of a true Christian.   The world is no friend to true grace : mark that !   A man may live for the world, and like the world, and escape persecution.   But if the world has nothing to say against you, it is a pretty sure sign that God has not much to say for you ; because if you do seek to live unto Christ Jesus you must go against the current of the world.

And now they are ready to let the news go forth ; and it is not long before it spreads through the highways of Babylon. The men of the city knew the man : knew that he would not vacillate. They knew that the old man with the grey locks would not turn to the right hand or the left : they knew that if his enemies caught him in that way, he would not deny his God or turn away from Him : they knew that he was going to be true to his God.

MORAL COURAGE.

Daniel was none of your sickly Christians of the nineteenth century : he was none of your weak-backed, none of your weak-kneed Christians : he had moral stamina and courage. I can imagine that aged white-haired Secretary of State sitting at his table going over the accounts of some of these rulers of provinces. Some of the timid, frightened Hebrews come to him, and say :

" Oh, Daniel, have you heard the latest news ? "

" No. What is it ? "

" What ! have you not been to the king's palace this morning ? "

"No ! I have not been to the palace to-day. What is the matter ? "

" Well, there is a conspiracy against you. A lot of those princes have induced King Darius to sign a decree that if any man shall call upon any God in his kingdom within thirty days he shall be thrown to the lions. Their object is to have you cast into the den. Now if you can only get out of the way for a little time—if you will just quit Babylon for thirty days— it will advance both your own and the public interest. You are the chief secretary and treasurer—in fact, you are the principal member of the government: you are an important man, and can do as you please. Well now, just you get out of Babylon. Or, if you will stay in Babylon, do not let any one catch you on your knees. In any case do not pray at the window which looks towards Jerusalem ; as you have been doing for the last fifty years. And if you will pray, close that window, draw a curtain over it ; shut the door, and stop up every crevice. People are sure to be about your house listening."

And some of our nineteenth century Christians would have advised after the same fashion :—" Cannot you find out some important business to be done down in Egypt, and so take a journey to Memphis ? or can you not think of something that needs being looked after in Syria, and so hurry off to Damascus? Or, surely you can make out there is a need for your going to Assyria, and you can make a stay at Nineveh. Or why not get as far as Jerusalem, and see what changes fifty or sixty years have wrought? Any way, just be out of Babylon for the next thirty days, so that your enemies may not catch you : for, depend upon it, they will all be on the watch. And, whatever you do, be sure they do not catch you on your knees."

How many men there are who are ashamed to be caught upon their knees! Many a man, if found upon his knees by the wife of his bosom, would jump right up and walk around the room as if he had no particular object in view. How many young men there are who come up from the country and enter upon city life, and have not the moral courage to go down on their knees before their .room-mates ! How many young men say, " Don't ask me to get down on my knees at this prayer-meeting." Men have not the moral courage to be seen praying. They lack moral courage. Ah ! thousands of men have been lost for lack of moral courage ; have been lost because at some critical moment they shrank from going on their knees, and being seen and known as being worshippers of God—as being on the Lord's side. Ah, the fact is—we are a pack of cowards : that is what we are. Shame on the Christianity of the nineteenth century ! it is a weak and sickly thing. Would to God that we had a host of men like Daniel living to-day !

I can picture that aged man, with his grey hairs upon him, listening to the words of these " miserable counsellors," who would tempt him to " trim," and " hedge," and shift—to " save his skin," as men say, at the cost of his conscience. And their counsel falls flat and dead. I can fancy how Daniel would receive a suggestion that he should even seemingly be ashamed of the God of his fathers. Will he be ashamed or afraid? Not likely! You know he will not; and I know he will not.

"They will be watching you; they will have their spies all around. But if you are determined to go on praying, shut up your window; close all your curtains; stop up the keyhole, so that no one can look through to see you on your knees, and so that no one can overhear a single word. Accommodate yourself just a little. Compromise just a little."

That is just the cry of the world to-day! It is, "Accommodate yourself to the times. Compromise just a little here; and deviate just a little there, just to suit the opinions and views of a mocking world." Do you think that Daniel, after having walked with God for half a century or more, is going to turn round like that? Ten thousand times, No!

True as steel, that old man goes to his room three times a day. Mark you, he had time to pray. There is many a business man to-day who will tell you he has no time to pray: his business is so pressing that he cannot call his family around him, and ask God to bless them. He is so busy that he cannot ask God to keep him and them from the temptations of the present life—the temptations of every day. "Business is so pressing." I am reminded of the words of an old Methodist minister: "If you have so much business to attend to that you have no time to pray, depend upon it you have more business on hand than God ever intended you should have." But look at this man. He had the whole, or nearly the whole, of the king's business to attend to. He was Prime Minister, Secretary of State, and Secretary of the Treasury, all in one. He had to attend to all his own work; and to give an eye to the work of lots of other men And yet he found time to pray: not just now and then, nor once in a way, not just when he happened to have a few moments to spare, mark you—but "three times a day." Yes, he could take up the words of the fifty-fifth Psalm, and say:

> " As for me, I will call upon God ;
> And the Lord shall save me.
> Evening, and morning, and at noon, will I pray and cry aloud ;
> And He shall hear my voice."

Busy as he was, he found time to pray.   And a man whose habit it is to call upon God saves time, instead of losing it. He has a clearer head, a more collected mind, and can act with more decision when circumstances require it.

So Daniel went to his room three times a day : he trod that path so often that the grass could not grow upon it.   I would be bound to say those plotters knew whereabouts he would be going to pray : they knew the place where Daniel's prayer was wont to be made ; and they were sure they should find him there at his usual hours.   And now again he has

> "a purpose firm,
> And dares to make it known."

He goes to pray as aforetime ; and *he has his windows open.* Like Paul, in later days, he " knew whom he had believed "; like Moses, he " saw Him who is invisible."   He knew whom he worshipped.   There was no need to trace back the church records for years to find out whether this man had ever made a profession of religion.   See him as he falls upon his knees. He is not careful to inquire whether there are any outsiders, or whether they can hear.   In tones not one atom softer or quieter than his custom, he pours out his prayer to the God of his life ; to the God of his people ; to the God of Abraham, Isaac, and Jacob.   He does not omit to pray for the king.   It is right to pray for our rulers.   If we cease praying for our rulers, our country will go to pieces.   The reason they are not better is oftentimes because we do not pray for them.   Does Daniel pray to Darius?   Not he !   He prays *for* Darius, but not *to* him.

There are men listening there near the open window : the **hundred and twenty** princes have taken **good care of that.**

They themselves are their own witnesses, and some of them gather together as listeners, so doing their own vile work If there had been any newspaper reporters in that day, how anxious they would have been to have got hold of every word of that prayer ! Give them the smallest chance ; and they would have taken it down, and telegraphed it all over the world, inside of twenty-four hours.

After Daniel has prayed, "and given thanks,"—"*given thanks*," mark that !—he goes out, and walks along the street with a firm step. He is undaunted. If it be the will of God that he shall pass from earth to heaven by the way of the den of lions, he is prepared for that. God's presence is with him. Like Enoch, he bore within himself this testimony—"that he pleased God."

> Do you see the Hebrew captive kneeling,
>   At morning, noon, and night, to pray ?
> In his chamber he remembers Zion,
>   Though in exile far away.
>
> Do not fear to tread the fiery furnace,
>   Nor shrink the lions' den to share ;
> For the God of Daniel will deliver,
>   He will send His angel there.
>
> Children of the living God, take courage,
>   Your great deliverance sweetly sing ;
> Set your faces toward the hill of Zion,
>   Thence to hail your coming King !

> Are your windows open toward Jerusalem,
>   Though as captives here " a little while " we stay ?
> For the coming of the King in His glory,
>   Are you watching day by day.

VII.

THE DEN OF LIONS.

"Then the king commanded, and they brought Daniel, and cast him
into the den of lions" (Dan. vi. 16).

HERE must have been great excitement in the city
then : all Babylon knew that this man was not
going to swerve. They knew very well that this old
statesman was a man of iron will ; and that it was
not at all likely he would yield. The lions' den had
few terrors to him. He would rather be in the lions' den with
God, than out of it without Him. And it is a thousand times
better, friends, to be in the lions' den with God, and hold to
principle—than to be out of it, and have money, but no principle. I pity those men who have gained their money dishonestly ; I pity those men who have obtained their positions
in life dishonestly ; I pity any politician who has acquired his
office dishonestly – how his conscience will lash him at times !
And how the Word of God lashes such ! "Your gold and
silver is cankered ; and the rust of them shall be a witness
against you, and *shall eat your flesh as it were fire.*" It does
not pay to be false ; it pays to be true. It is best to be
honest ; even if it means having very little money in our
pocket, and very little position in the world. It is best to
have God with us, and to know that we are on the right side.

I venture to say that man Daniel was worth more than any
other **man** Darius had in his empire—yes, worth more than

forty thousand men who wanted to get him out of the way. He was true to the king. He prayed for him; he loved him; and he did for that king everything he could that did not conflict with the law of his God.

And now the spies rush off to the king, and cry,

"O Darius, live for ever! Do you know there is a man in your kingdom who will not obey you?"

"A man who won't obey me! Who is he?"

"Why, that man Daniel. That Hebrew whom you set over us He persists in calling upon his God."

And the moment they mention the name of Daniel, a frown arises upon the king's brow; and the thought flashes into his mind: "Ah! I have made a mistake: I ought never to have signed that decree I might have known that Daniel would never 'call' upon me. I know very well whom he serves: he serves the God of his fathers." So, instead of blaming Daniel he blames himself: instead of condemning Daniel he condemns himself. And then he casts about in his mind as to how he could manage to preserve him unharmed. All that day, if you could have looked into the palace, you would have seen the king walking up and down the halls and corridors, greatly troubled with the thought that this man must lose his life before the sun sets on that Chaldæan plain; for if Daniel were not in the lions' den by sundown the law of the Medes and Persians would be broken: and come what will, that law must be observed and kept.

Darius loved Daniel; and he sought in his heart to deliver him. All day he sought for some plan by which he might save Daniel, and yet preserve the Median law unbroken. But he did not love Daniel as much as your King loved you: he did not love him as much as Christ loved us: for if he had he would have proposed to have gone into the lions' den in his stead. Let us remember that Christ "tasted death" for us. I can imagine those plotters having a suspicion as to the king's feelings; and saying to him, "If you break the law which **you** yourself have made, respect for the laws of the Medes and Persians will be gone: your subjects will no longer obey you; and your kingdom will depart from you." So Darius is at last compelled to give him up; and he speaks the word for the officers to seize him and take him to the den. And his enemies would take good care that the den is filled with the hungriest beasts in Babylon.

You might have seen those officers going out to bind that old man with the white flowing hair: they march to his dwelling; and they bind his hands together. And those Chaldæan soldiers lead captive the man who a few hours before ranked next to the king; the noblest statesman Babylon had ever possessed. They guard him along the way that leads to the lions' den. Look at him as he is led along the streets. He treads with a firm and steady step, bearing himself like a conqueror. He trembles not. His knees are firm: they do not smite together. The light of heaven shines in his calm face. And all heaven is interested in that aged man. Disgraced down here upon earth, he is the most popular man in heaven. Angels are delighted in him: how they love him up there! He had stood firm; he had not deviated; he had not turned away from the God of the Bible. And he walks with a giant's tread to the entrance of the lions' den; and they cast him in. They roll a great stone to the mouth of the den; and the king puts his seal upon it. And so the law is kept.

Daniel is cast into the den; but the angel of God flies down, and God's servant lights unharmed at the bottom. The lions' mouths are stopped: they are as harmless as lambs. And if you could have looked into that den, you would have found a man as calm as a summer evening. I do not doubt that at his wonted hour of prayer he knelt down as if he had been in his own chamber. And if he could get the

points of the compass in that den, he prayed with his face
toward Jerusalem. He loved that city; he loved the temple:
and probably with his face toward the city of Jerusalem, he
prayed and gave thanks. And later on I can imagine him just
laying his head on one of the lions, and going to sleep: and if
that were so, no one in Babylon slept more sweetly than Daniel
in the den of lions.

But there was one man in Babylon who had no rest that
night. If you could have looked into the king's palace, you
would have seen one man in great trouble. Darius did not
have in his musicians to play to him that night. Away with
music and singing! There was no feast that night: he could
eat nothing. The servants brought him dainty food; but he
had no appetite for it. He felt troubled: he could not sleep.
He had put in that den of lions the best man in his kingdom;
and he upbraided himself for it. He said to himself, "How
could I have been a party to such an act as that?"

And early in the morning — probably in the grey dawn,
before the sun has risen—the men of Babylon could have
heard the wheels of the king's chariot rolling over the pavement; and King Darius might have been seen driving in hot
haste to the lions' den. I see him alight from his chariot in
eager haste, and hear him cry down through the mouth of
the den: "O Daniel, servant of the living God, is thy God,
whom thou servest continually, able to deliver thee from the
lions?"

Hark! a voice gives answer—why, it is like a resurrection
voice—and from the depths come up to the king's ear the
words of Daniel: "O king, live for ever! My God hath sent
His angel, and hath shut the lions' mouths, that they have not
hurt me: forasmuch as before Him innocency was found in
me; and also before thee, O king, have I done no hurt."

The lions could not harm him. The very hairs of his head
were numbered. I tell you, that whenever a man stands by

God, God will stand by him   It was well for Daniel that he
did not swerve.   Oh, how his name shines!   What a blessed
character he was!

The king gives command that Daniel should be taken up
out of the den.   And, as he reaches the top, I fancy I see them
embracing one another; and that then Daniel mounts the king's
chariot, and is driven back with him to the royal palace.   There
were two happy men in Babylon that morning.   Most likely
they sat down at meat together, thankful and rejoicing.

"No manner of hurt was found upon him."   The God who
had preserved Shadrach, Meshach, and Abednego, in the fiery
furnace, so that "no smell of fire had passed on them," had
preserved Daniel from the jaws of the lions.

But Daniel's accusers fared very differently.   So to speak,
they "digged a pit for him ; and are fallen into it themselves."
The king orders that Daniel's accusers shall be delivered to
the same ordeal.   And they were cast into the den ; "and the
lions had the mastery of them, and brake all their bones in
pieces or ever they came at the bottom of the den."

Young men, let us come out from the world; let us trample
it under our feet ; let us be true to God; let us stand in rank,
and keep step, and fight boldly for our King!   And our
"crowning time" shall come by and by.   Yes, the reward will
come by and by; and then it may perhaps be said of one,
or another, of us: "O man, greatly beloved!"   Young men,
your moral character is more than money, mark that!   It is
worth more than the honour of the world: that is fleeting,
and will soon be gone.   It is worth more than earthly position :
that is transient, and will soon be gone.   But to have God
with you, and to be with God—what a grand position!   It is
an eternal inheritance.

I should like to say a few more words about Daniel.   If
you will refer to the tenth chapter, you will read that an angel

came to him, and told him he was "a man greatly beloved." Another angel had on a previous occasion brought him a similar message. Many are of opinion that the one described in the tenth chapter as appearing to Daniel is none other than the one "like unto the Son of Man," who visited John when he was banished to the Isle of Patmos. People thought that John was sent off to that island by himself; but no ! the angel of God was with him. And so it was with Daniel, taken from his own country and his own people. Here in this chapter we read: "Then I lifted up mine eyes, and looked ; and behold a certain man clothed in linen, whose loins were girded with fine gold of Uphaz. . . . . And he said unto me, O Daniel, a man greatly beloved, understand the words that I speak unto thee ; and stand upright : for unto thee am I now sent."

It was Daniel's need that brought this angel from the glory-land. And it was the Son of God right by his side in that city of Babylon. As I said before, that was the second time the word had come to him that he was "greatly beloved." Aye, and even *three times* did a messenger come from the throne of God to tell him this.

I love that precious verse in the eleventh chapter : "The people that do know their God shall be strong, and do exploits." And also those two verses of the twelfth chapter : "Many of them that sleep in the dust of the earth shall awake : some to everlasting life ; and some to shame and everlasting contempt. And they that be wise shall shine as the brightness of the firmament ; and they that turn many to righteousness, as the stars for ever and ever."

This was the consolation the angel bore to Daniel ; and great consolation it was. The fact concerning all of us is that we like to shine. There is no doubt about that Every mother likes her child to shine. If her boy shines at school by getting to the head of his class, the proud mother tells all the neighbours ; and she has a right to do so.

But it is not the great of this world who will shine the brightest. For a few years they may shed bright light : but they go out in darkness ; they have no inner light. Shining for a time, they go out in the blackness of darkness   Where are the great men who did not know Daniel's God?   Did they shine long ?   Why, we know of Nebuchadnezzar and the rest of them scarcely anything, except as they fill in the story about these humble men of God.   We are not told that statesmen shall shine : they may for a few days or years; but they are soon forgotten.   Look at those great ones who passed away in the days of Daniel.   How wise in council they were ! how mighty and victorious over many nations ! what gods upon earth they were !   Yet their names are forgotten, and written in the sand.   Philosophers, falsely so-called, do they live ? Behold men of science—scientific men, they call themselves— going down into the bowels of the earth, hammering away at some rock, and trying to make it talk against the voice of God.   They shall go down to death by and by ; and their names shall rot.   But the man of God shines.   Yes, it is he who shall shine as the stars for ever and ever.   This Daniel has been gone for 2,500 years ; but still increasing millions read of his life and actions.   And so it shall be to the end. He will only get better known and better loved ; he will only shine the brighter as the world grows older.   Of a truth, "they that be wise " and "turn many to righteousness " shall shine on, like stars, to eternity.

And this blessed, thrice blessed, happiness, of shining in the glory, is like all the blessings of God's kingdom, for every one.   Even without the least claim to education or refinement you can shine if you will.   A poor working man, or a poor sailor before the mast, can shine for ever, if he only works for the King-dom of God.   The Bible does not say the great shall shine, but "they that turn many to righteousness."   A false impression has got hold of many of God's people.   They have formed the idea that only a few can speak on behalf of God. If anything is to be done for the souls of men, nine-tenths of the people say, " Oh, the ministers must do it." It does not enter into the thoughts of many people that they have any part in the matter. It is the devil's work to keep Christians from the blessed privilege of winning souls to God. ANY ONE CAN DO THIS WORK.

Do you not see how that little mountain rill keeps swelling till it carries everything before it? Little trickling streams have run into it till now, a mighty river, it has great cities on its banks, and the commerce of all nations floating on its waters. So when a single soul is won to Christ you cannot see the result. A single one multiplies to a thousand ; and the thousand into ten thousand. Perhaps a million shall be the fruit. We cannot tell. We only know that the Christian who has turned " many to righteousness" shall indeed shine for ever and ever. Look at those poor, unlettered fishermen, the disciples of Jesus. They were not learned men, but they were great in winning souls. And there is not a child but can work for God.

The one thing that keeps people from working for God is that they have not the desire to do so. If a man has this desire God soon qualifies him. And what we want is God's qualification : it must come from Him.

In our large meetings there are frequently three thousand Christians present. Would it be too much to expect if these were living in communion with Christ that they should each lead one soul to the Lord within a month ? The Son of God gave His life for them—shall they refuse to work for Him when He supplies the needed power ? What results should we see in souls saved if every one did his or her work. How many times have I watched at the close of a meeting to see if Christians would speak to the sorrowing ones. If we only had open eyed watchers for souls there would be multitudes of inquirers where now there are individual cases. Every church would need an inquiry meeting after every gospel service, and these inquiry rooms would be crowded. These inquiring ones are at every meeting, just anxious to have warm-hearted Christians lead them to Christ. They are timid, but will always listen to one speaking to them about Christ. Let the prayer of every Christian be, "Oh God, give me souls for my hire." What would be the result if this were the case with us? Multitudes would be sending up shouts of praise to God, and making heaven glad. Where there is an anxious sinner, there is the place for the Christian.

"WHAT ART THOU DOING?"

" What art *thou* doing, Christian?
  Is it work for Christ thy Lord?
Art thou winning many sinners
  By thy life, thy pen, thy word?
When the solemn question com-
    eth,
  What will thine answer be?
Canst thou point to something
    finished?—
  Saying—"Lord, my work for
    Thee!"

" What doest thou in service?—
  Art thou taking active part?
Are life and tongue in earnest,
  Outflow of loving heart?
Or art thou idly gazing
  While others toil and sow,
Content with simply praising
  The earnestness they show?

" What doest thou, redeemed one,
  Child of a mighty King?
What glory to thy Father
  Doth thy princely bearing
    bring?
If no one brought Him honour,
  And no one gave Him praise,
To thee it appertaineth
  The pæan-note to raise.

" What doest thou here? Where-
    ever
  Thine earthly lot be cast,
Oh, let each hour and moment
  In gladsome work be passed!
Here! thou may'st do a life-
    work;
  Here! thou may'st win a crown,
Starlit and gem-surrounded,
  To cast before the throne."

EVA TRAVERS POOLE.

www.ingramcontent.com/pod-product-compliance
Lightning Source LLC
Chambersburg PA
CBHW021349090426
42742CB00008B/793